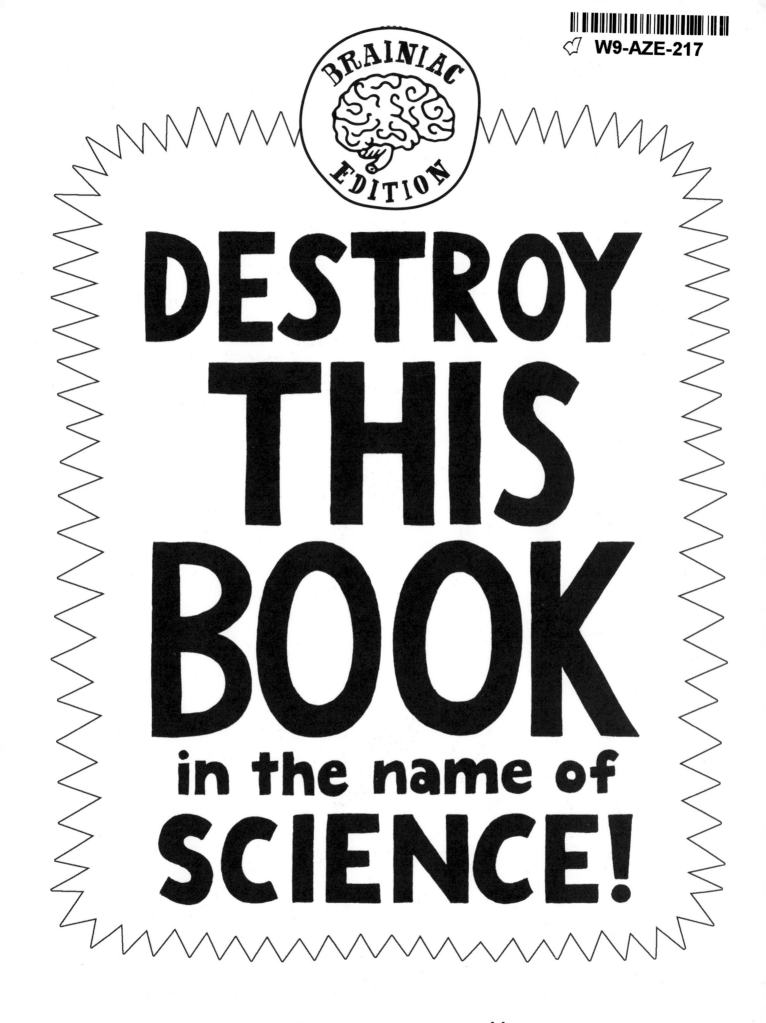

DESTROY
THIS
BOOK
in the name of
SCIENCE!

BRAINIAC
EDITION

W9-AZE-217

CROWN BOOKS FOR YOUNG READERS ♕ NEW YORK

WRITTEN, DRAWN AND CREATED BY
MIKE BARFIELD

WITH A LITTLE HELP FROM THESE GENIUSES . . .

ISAAC NEWTON — MARIE CURIE — ALBERT EINSTEIN

AND DON'T FORGET THESE ONES, EITHER . . .

MIKE BARFIELD — YOU — YOU IN THE FUTURE

Visit us on the Web! rhcbooks.com

Educators and librarians, for a variety of teaching tools, visit us at RHTeachersLibrarians.com

Library of Congress Cataloging-in-Publication Data is available upon request.

ISBN 978-1-5247-7194-2

MANUFACTURED IN CHINA

10 9 8 7 6 5 4 3

First American Edition

CONTENTS

ABOUT THE AUTHOR

Mike Barfield is a writer, cartoonist, poet and performer who has worked in TV and radio. When he isn't busy writing and drawing, he puts his university science degree to work performing humorous science-based shows and workshops at schools, libraries, festivals, museums and bookshops.

INTRODUCTION

Crammed inside this book you will find lots of projects to press out, cut out, stick, fold, color in and scribble on.

Your mission is to **DESTROY** this book by completing all of the experiments in it (and by having tons of fun in the process). There are bite-sized facts to feast upon and nuggets of scientific information to digest, too.

You don't need any expensive or hard-to-find craft supplies to complete the projects. Most of the models require glue and tape to build them. You can also use pencils and pens to customize or personalize the designs and to color them in.

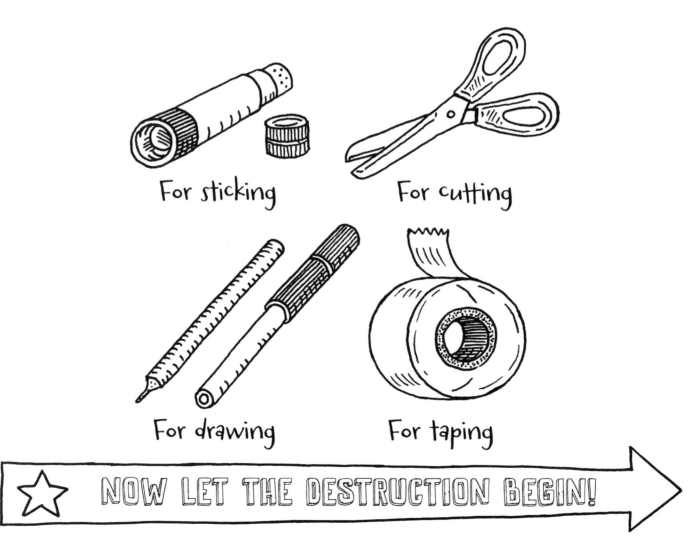

For sticking

For cutting

For drawing

For taping

☆ NOW LET THE DESTRUCTION BEGIN! ➡️

GET SHIRTY!

Dr. Hermann has a new white shirt with squares on it. However, he decides it is too white, so he colors all the squares black. Now when he wears it people tell him his shirt has spots. Is this true?

Color all the squares black.

WOW!

WHAT HAPPENS IF YOU TRY TO STARE DIRECTLY AT EACH SPOT?

WHAT'S THE SCIENCE? →

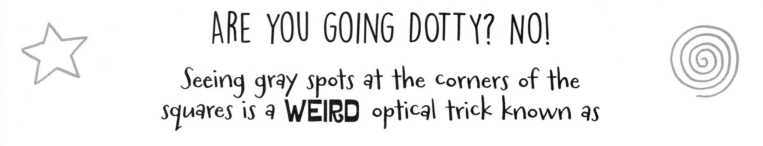

Seeing gray spots at the corners of the squares is a **WEIRD** optical trick known as

THE HERMANN GRID ILLUSION.

It is named after the German scientist Ludimar Hermann, who first described it in 1870, after noticing the effect in a book illustration.

YOU CAN GET SPOTS WITH WHITE SQUARES, TOO.

Color all the grid lines black. You should see more spots. But what color are they?

1. Color the squares in this grid red. What color are the spots this time?

2. Next, color the lines yellow. Now what color are the spots you see?

Amazingly, no one is quite sure why our eyes produce this illusion. Some say this rear part of the brain is involved.

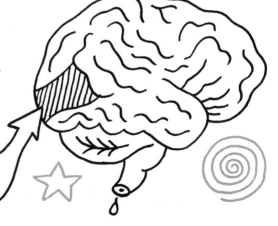

PRIMARY VISUAL CORTEX

LIGHT UP THE SKY
FABULOUS FIREWORK COLORING

The chemicals inside fireworks produce different colors when they burn.
Can you color the picture according to these chemical symbols?

Ba
Barium/GREEN

Sr
Strontium/RED

Mg
Magnesium/WHITE

Na
Sodium/YELLOW

Ca
Calcium/ORANGE

Cu
Copper/BLUE

K
Potassium/PINK

7

BUILD YOUR OWN BRAINIAC (BYOB)
NO. 1: ALBERT EINSTEIN

Albert Einstein is the world's **MOST FAMOUS SCIENCE SUPERSTAR.**

Born in Germany in 1879, young Al became interested in science when his dad gave him a compass and he wondered why it always pointed north.*

*The answer is because of the Earth's magnetic field.

Albert was brilliant at math and physics. He won the Nobel Prize in 1921 for his work on light and electricity.

Einstein's most famous scientific equation states:

$$E = MC^2$$

(E = M x C SQUARED)

E = ENERGY RELEASED, M = MASS
C = THE SPEED OF LIGHT

This famous formula explains why the sun shines and why atomic bombs go

BOOM!

After he died, Albert's brain was removed and kept in a jar.

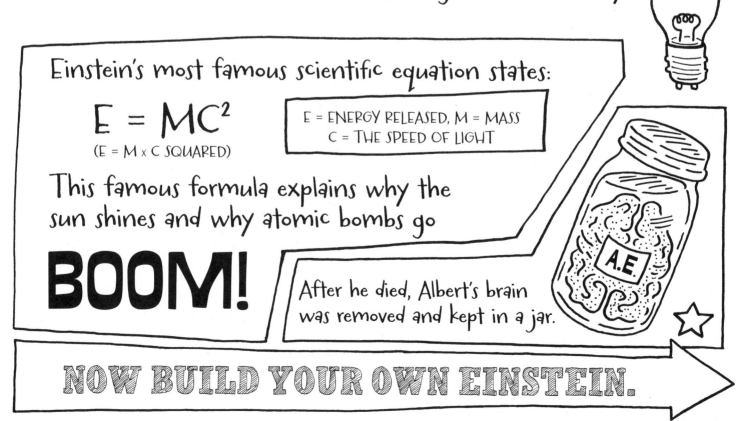

NOW BUILD YOUR OWN EINSTEIN.

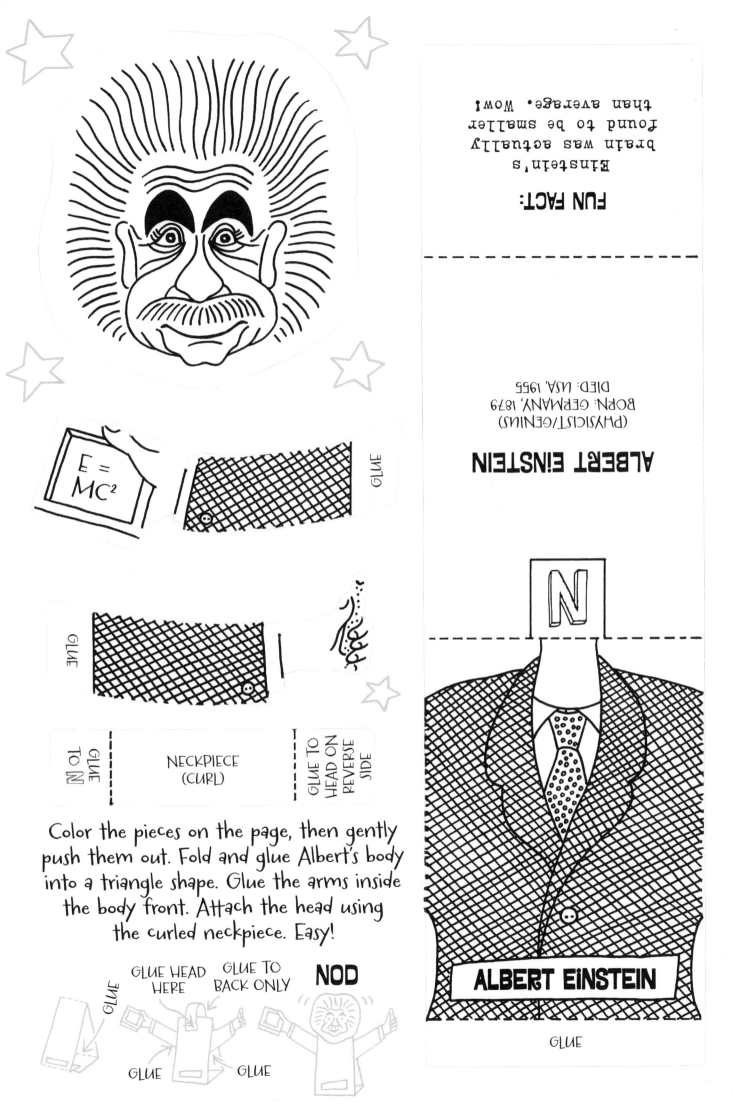

E = MC²

GLUE

GLUE

GLUE TO N

NECKPIECE (CURL)

GLUE TO HEAD ON REVERSE SIDE

Color the pieces on the page, then gently push them out. Fold and glue Albert's body into a triangle shape. Glue the arms inside the body front. Attach the head using the curled neckpiece. Easy!

GLUE HEAD HERE   GLUE TO BACK ONLY   **NOD**

GLUE

GLUE   GLUE

FUN FACT:

Einstein's brain was actually found to be smaller than average. Wow!

DIED: USA, 1955
BORN: GERMANY, 1879
(PHYSICIST/GENIUS)

ALBERT EINSTEIN

N

ALBERT EINSTEIN

GLUE

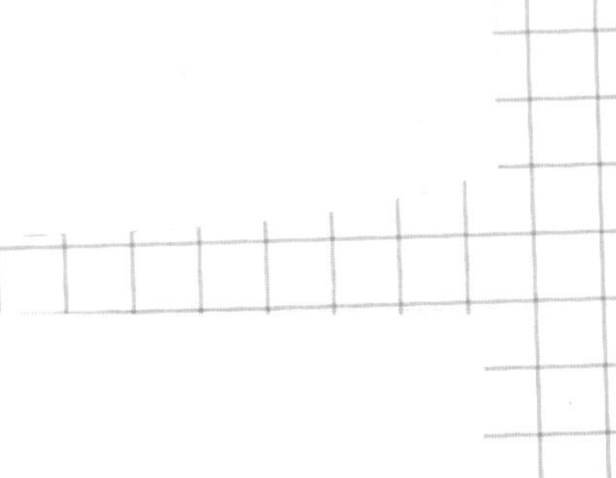

The most
famous
photograph
of Albert was
taken on his
72nd birthday in
March 1951. Tired
of posing for pictures,
he stuck out his tongue.

TURBO TURTLES

Press out and make the sea-turtle racers. Float them in a shallow bath of fresh, cold water, then drop a blob of liquid soap into each keyhole-shaped slot and see what happens.

Color in the turtles.

WOW!

LOGGERHEAD TURTLE

FUN FACT: Loggerhead turtles cry to get rid of salt from their bodies.

GLUE CLOSED

FOLD UNDER AND GLUE SHUT

DONE!

GREEN SEA TURTLE

FUN FACT: Green sea turtles aren't usually green. They are often black or brown.

DRIP SOAP INTO THESE SLOTS

WHAT'S THE SCIENCE?

WHY DO THE TURTLES RACE?

Water molecules stick together to form a sort of "skin" at the surface. This is called surface tension. Adding soap means the water molecules at the rear of the turtle pull less strongly on it than those at the front. As a result, the turtles go **ZOOM!**

This is called the **MARANGONI EFFECT.** It stops once there is soap all over the water's surface. So, to repeat the experiment, dry off your turtle and use fresh, clean water.

YOU SHOULD HAVE SEEN THIS:

1. Add soap.

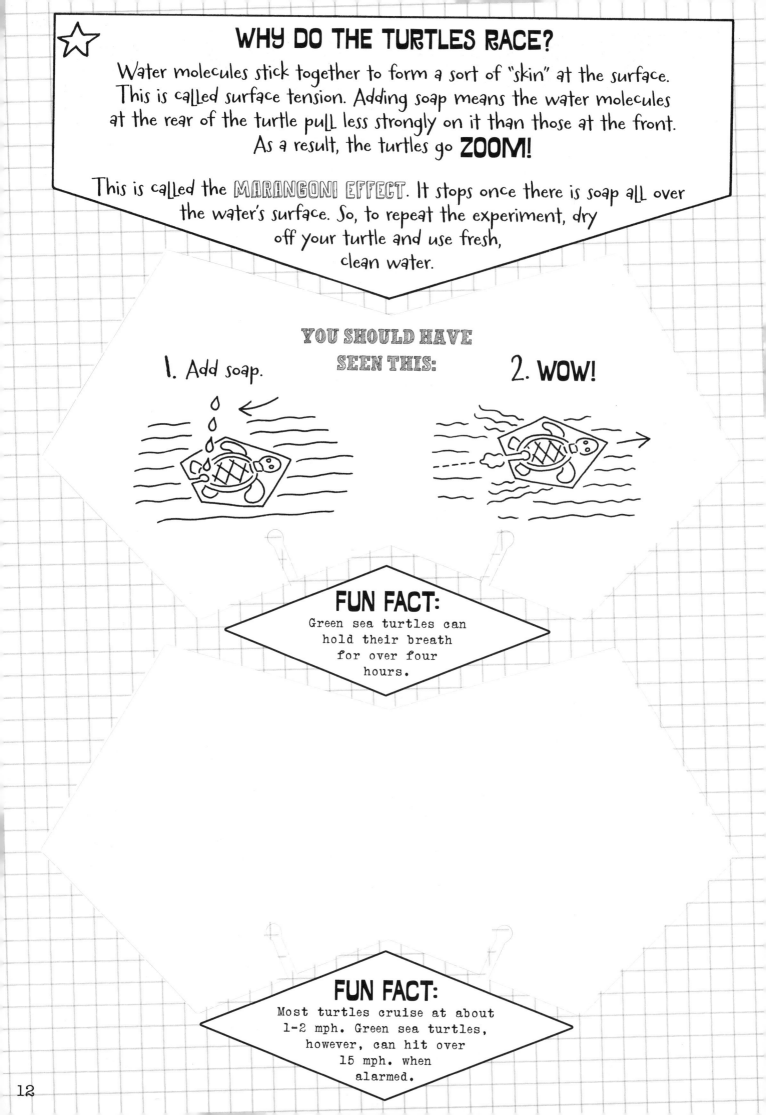

2. WOW!

FUN FACT:
Green sea turtles can hold their breath for over four hours.

FUN FACT:
Most turtles cruise at about 1-2 mph. Green sea turtles, however, can hit over 15 mph. when alarmed.

PIPE UP! (AND DOWN)

MAKE A MUSICAL SLIDE WHISTLE.

Carefully press out the rectangle below and roll it around a smooth, 6-in.-long pencil as directed below.

Roll it neatly around the pencil to form a tube. (This text will be on the inside of the pipe.)

Glue the final edge to fix it in place, leaving the pencil inside.

The pencil should fit snugly, but still be able to slide up and down the tube smoothly.

Glue the press-out piece (below) over the point of the pencil to form a handle.

FOLD DOWN

GLUE OVER PENCIL POINT

Done!

GLUE

Finished pipe ↗

Handle piece ↗

BUT HOW DO YOU PLAY IT?

It's simple to play your whistle. Purse your lips and blow over the open end to produce a note.

Moving the pencil upward makes the space inside the tube smaller and produces a higher-pitched note. Moving the pencil down creates a larger space, producing a lower note.

HIGH NOTE

LOW NOTE

CAN YOU PLAY A TUNE?

The science of sound is called acoustics. Blowing across the pipe makes the air inside vibrate. The faster the air vibrates, the higher the note. The vibrations reach our ears and we hear them as sound.

BENHAM'S TOP

⭐ ⭐

CAN YOU BELIEVE YOUR EYES? 👁️ 👁️

1. Press out the three pieces of the top.

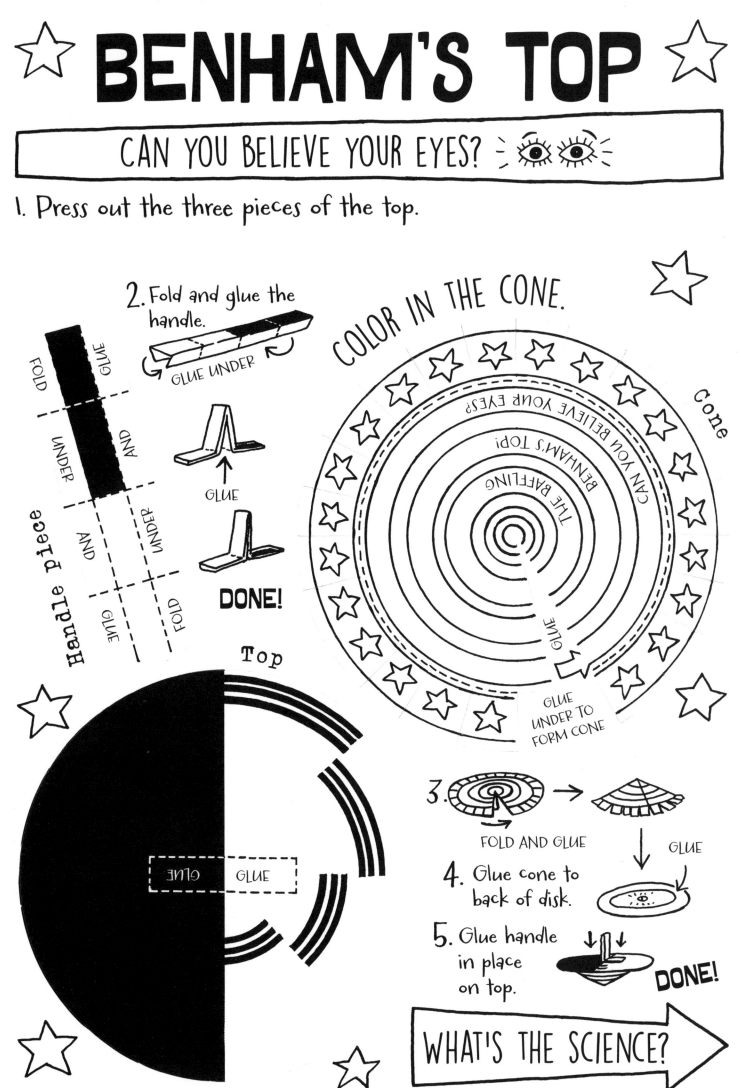

2. Fold and glue the handle.

GLUE UNDER

GLUE

DONE!

Handle piece
FOLD — GLUE — UNDER — AND — AND — UNDER — AND — UNDER — GLUE — FOLD

COLOR IN THE CONE.

Cone

CAN YOU BELIEVE YOUR EYES?

BENHAM'S TOP!

THE BAFFLING

GLUE

GLUE UNDER TO FORM CONE

Top

GLUE   GLUE

3. → FOLD AND GLUE → GLUE

4. Glue cone to back of disk.

5. Glue handle in place on top.

DONE!

WHAT'S THE SCIENCE?

SPINNING THE TOP SHOULD PRODUCE PALE BANDS OF COLOR KNOWN AS FECHNER ("FECK-NER") COLORS, AFTER THE GERMAN PHYSICIST WHO FIRST DESCRIBED THEM IN 1838. NOT EVERYONE SEES THE SAME COLORS, AND SOME PEOPLE DON'T SEE ANY COLORS AT ALL.

Gustav Fechner
(1801–1887)

Charles Benham
(1860–1929)

PUT GLUE ON HERE TO ATTACH CONE TO DISK

FUN FACT:

Human eyes are about the size of a cherry tomato.

YUM

YUM

Actual size

Each eye contains over 120 million cells that can detect light.

PUT GLUE ON HERE TO ATTACH CONE TO DISK

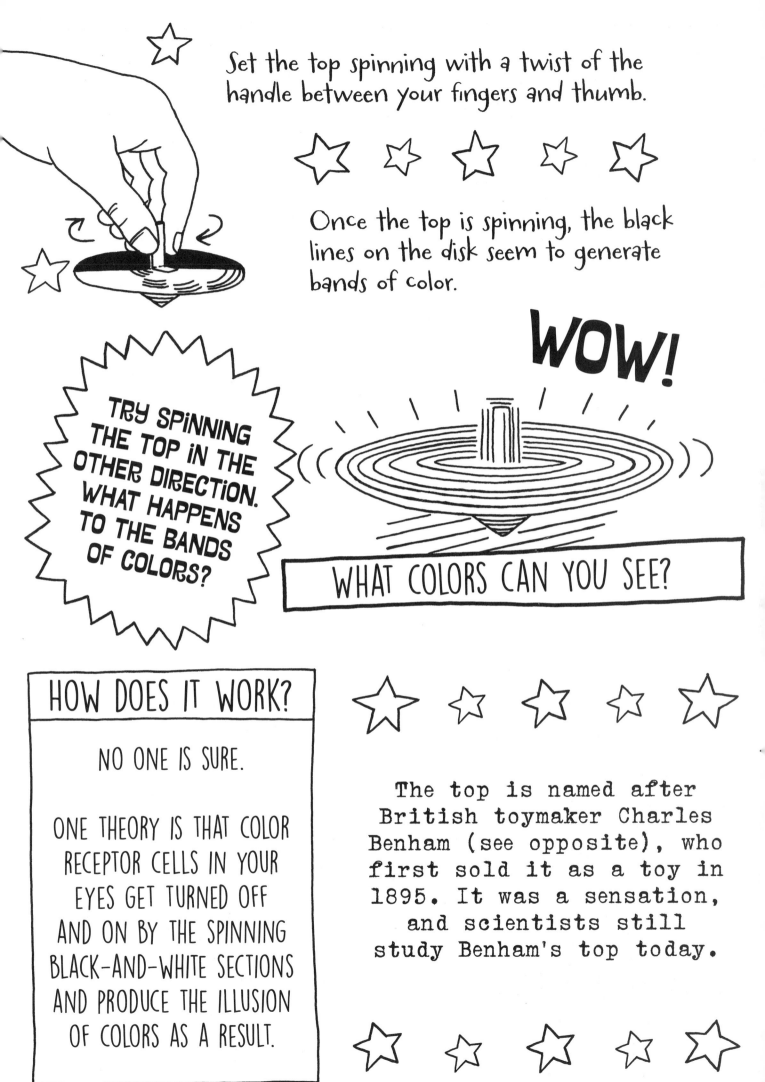

Set the top spinning with a twist of the handle between your fingers and thumb.

Once the top is spinning, the black lines on the disk seem to generate bands of color.

WOW!

TRY SPINNING THE TOP IN THE OTHER DIRECTION. WHAT HAPPENS TO THE BANDS OF COLORS?

WHAT COLORS CAN YOU SEE?

HOW DOES IT WORK?

NO ONE IS SURE.

ONE THEORY IS THAT COLOR RECEPTOR CELLS IN YOUR EYES GET TURNED OFF AND ON BY THE SPINNING BLACK-AND-WHITE SECTIONS AND PRODUCE THE ILLUSION OF COLORS AS A RESULT.

The top is named after British toymaker Charles Benham (see opposite), who first sold it as a toy in 1895. It was a sensation, and scientists still study Benham's top today.

WHO IS IN THE ZOO?

THERE'S CONFUSION AT THE ZOO. THE ZOOKEEPERS CAN'T AGREE ON THE IDENTITY OF THE NEW ARRIVAL.

Complete the connect-the-dots puzzle below to see if you can help them decide if it's a penguin or a rabbit.

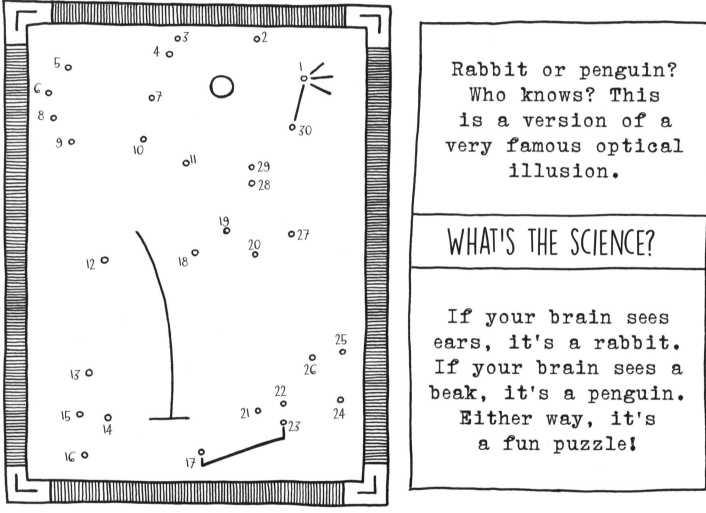

Rabbit or penguin? Who knows? This is a version of a very famous optical illusion.

WHAT'S THE SCIENCE?

If your brain sees ears, it's a rabbit. If your brain sees a beak, it's a penguin. Either way, it's a fun puzzle!

Humans aren't the only animals that can struggle with shapes. Color in this bird to make it a solid shape.

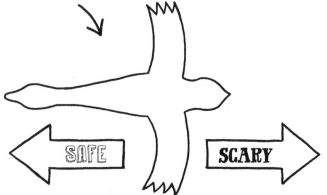

SAFE

SCARY

If you imagine it flying to the left, it has the outline of a harmless goose. Flying to the right, however, it looks like a hunting hawk.

AFTERIMAGES

If you stare at the same thing for too long, your eyes will start to produce a "phantom" image of it called an afterimage. This becomes apparent when you look away and blink a few times. Try it out with these black-and-white examples.

Stare at the cross in the left-hand box for 30 seconds, then concentrate on the cross on the right.

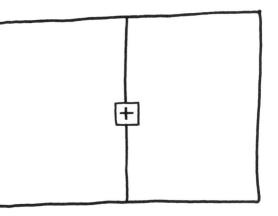

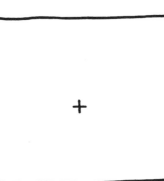

Did you notice how the black and white tones reverse?

Using the same method, can you turn a black cat in the snow into a ghostly gray cat in the dark?

Here's Science Superstar Albert Einstein. Stare at the hair box for 30 seconds, then switch to the face box. What happens?

DRAW YOUR OWN BLACK-AND-WHITE PICTURES IN HERE.

You can also get colored afterimages. Different colors produce a variety of results known as "inverted" colors.

COLOR THE CRAZY FRUITS AS SUGGESTED, STARE AT EACH FOR 30 SECONDS, THEN LOOK IN THE FRUIT BOWL.

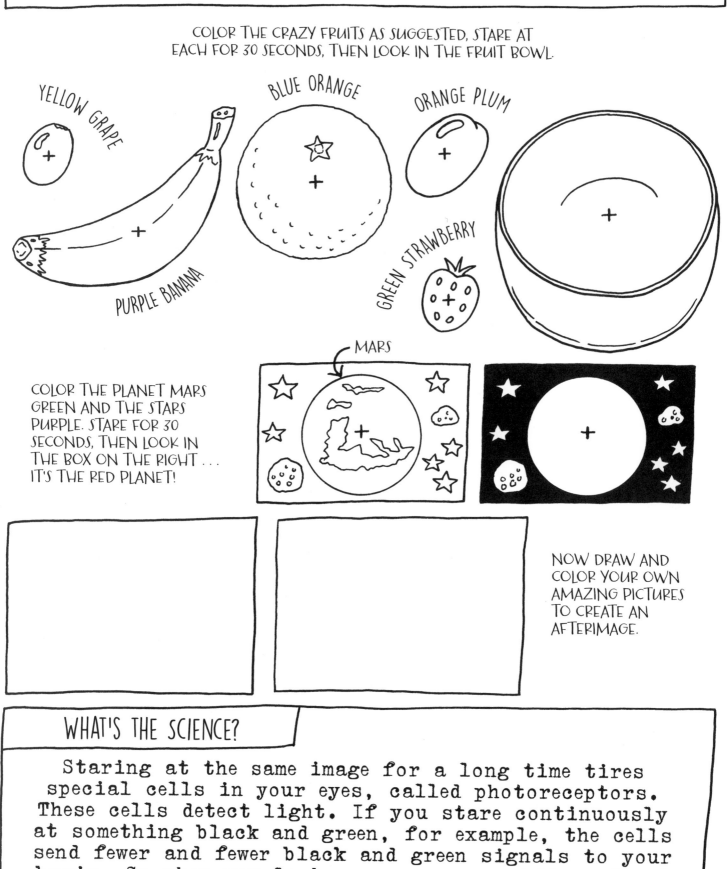

YELLOW GRAPE

BLUE ORANGE

ORANGE PLUM

PURPLE BANANA

GREEN STRAWBERRY

COLOR THE PLANET MARS GREEN AND THE STARS PURPLE. STARE FOR 30 SECONDS, THEN LOOK IN THE BOX ON THE RIGHT . . . IT'S THE RED PLANET!

MARS

NOW DRAW AND COLOR YOUR OWN AMAZING PICTURES TO CREATE AN AFTERIMAGE.

WHAT'S THE SCIENCE?

Staring at the same image for a long time tires special cells in your eyes, called photoreceptors. These cells detect light. If you stare continuously at something black and green, for example, the cells send fewer and fewer black and green signals to your brain. So when you look away, you see white and red shades (the inverted colors of black and green).

FLOWER POWER

Color the flower petals using crayons or waterproof markers, then carefully cut around the flower with scissors. Fold the outer petals into the center along the dotted lines. Place the flower on cold, clean water and watch what happens. It's blooming!

FOLD PETALS INTO CENTER. 1.

PLACE ON WATER. 2.

Actual lily flowers can be twice this size.

Giant waterlily (Victoria amazonica)

WHAT'S THE SCIENCE?

The flower floats because paper is less dense than water. Shortly after you place it on the surface of the water, water molecules enter microscopic gaps in the paper by a process called capillary action. As fibers in the paper get wet, they swell and get bigger, pushing open the petals.

FUN FACT:
The giant waterlily grows leaves up to 10 feet wide. In fact, they are so big they can support a child.

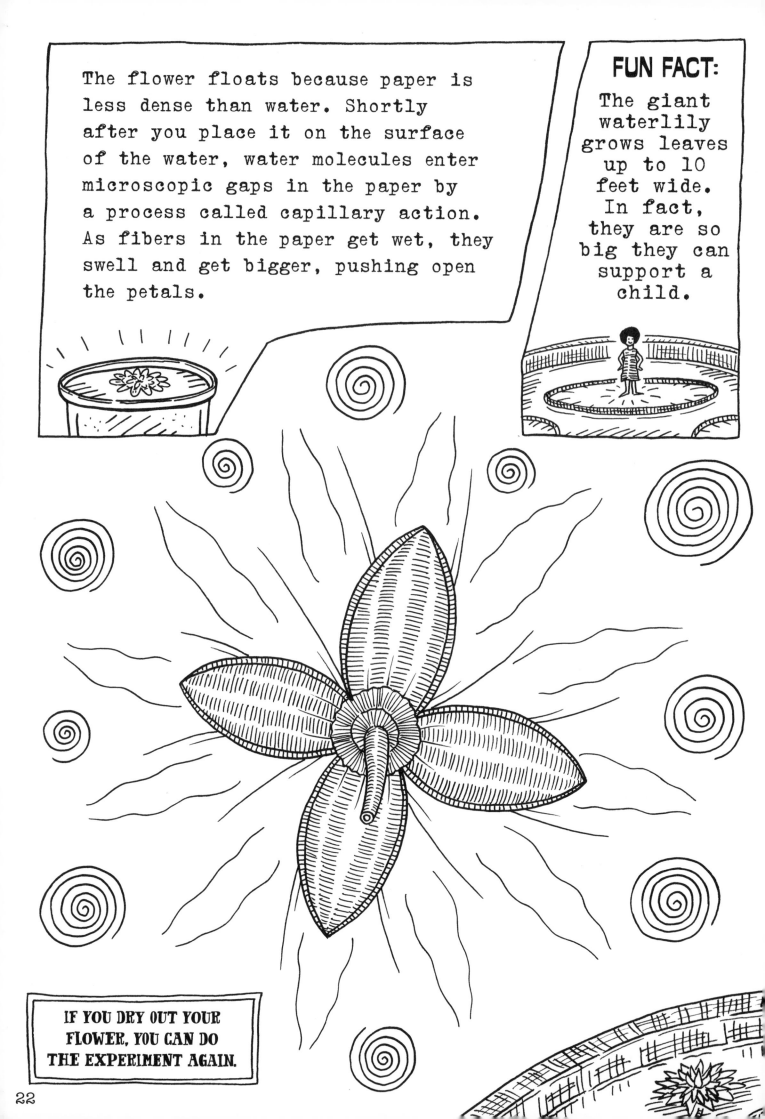

IF YOU DRY OUT YOUR FLOWER, YOU CAN DO THE EXPERIMENT AGAIN.

TRAIN YOUR BRAIN

Did you know you were born a computer programmer? From birth, you have programmed your brain to run your body—solving problems and moving muscles.

Using a pencil—and making sure to stay inside the lines—time how long it takes you to solve brain maze A. It should be fairly easy.

Next, place a small mirror on the page and try to complete maze B by only looking in the mirror. WARNING! It's hard.

WHAT'S THE SCIENCE?

The mirror reverses how your brain sees the world. As a result, you now have to think harder and longer about how to move your pencil.

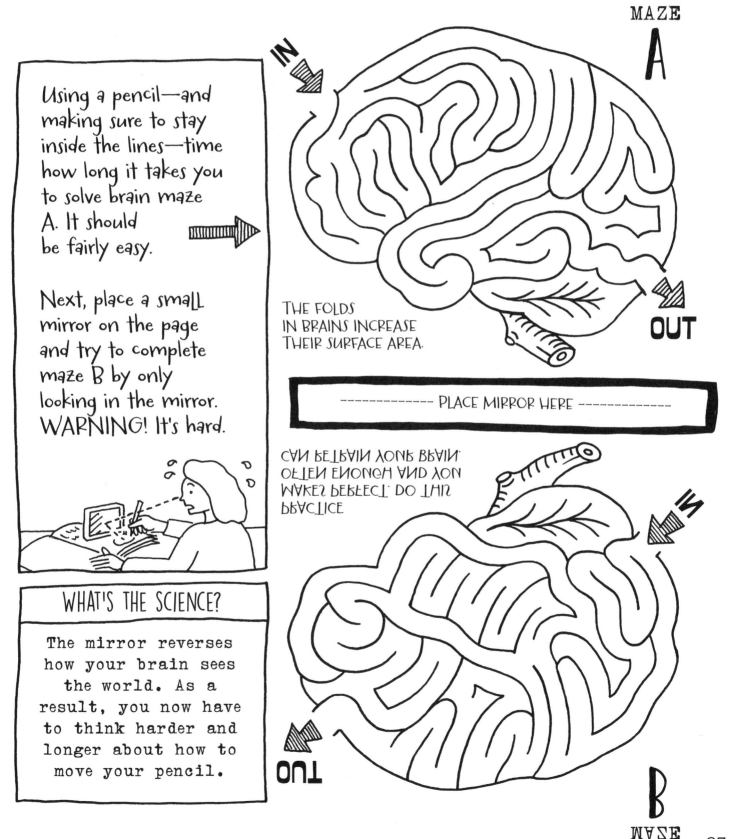

MAZE A

IN

OUT

THE FOLDS IN BRAINS INCREASE THEIR SURFACE AREA.

-------------- PLACE MIRROR HERE --------------

PRACTICE. DO THIS OFTEN ENOUGH AND YOU MAKES PERFECT. DO THIS CAN RETRAIN YOUR BRAIN.

IN

OUT

MAZE B

NO. 2: SIR ISAAC NEWTON

Sir Isaac Newton was a world-famous Science Superstar, born in England in 1643. His mom wanted him to run the family farm, but instead Isaac grew up to be a truly great scientist.

Isaac daringly carved his name into a stone windowsill at his school.

I Newton

In his lifetime, Isaac explored many areas of science and math. One famous story is about how he started thinking about GRAVITY when an apple fell from a branch above him.

Isaac wondered what made the apple fall down rather than sideways. He decided that it was attracted to the massive center of the Earth by a force called gravity.

NOW BUILD A BALANCING ISAAC.

Ever since Newton, scientists have struggled to explain what gravity is and what causes it. The latest theory is that gravity is the result of matter bending the invisible fabric of the universe. **WOW!**

BLACK HOLE

SPACE-TIME

INSTRUCTIONS

Press out the head of Sir Isaac, and tape two small coins on the back of his wig, as shown. Press out and make the pointy stand to balance his head on.

Stand

GLUE

FOLD AND GLUE TO MAKE THE STAND

TAPE COINS ON BACK

BALANCE ON STAND

ATTACH TWO IDENTICAL COINS TO THE SPACES UNDERNEATH.

Head

WHAT'S THE SCIENCE?

Sir Isaac's head balances because the pointy stand supports its

CENTER OF GRAVITY.

An object's center of gravity is the place where all its mass seems to be concentrated. For humans, this is roughly at a point that's level with their belly button.

WOBBLE!

You can also try balancing Isaac on your finger.

SIR ISAAC'S CENTER OF GRAVITY WILL BE CLOSE TO THIS POINT.

TAPE COIN HERE

TAPE COIN HERE

FUN FACT: Sir Isaac chose two crossed shinbones as his coat of arms.

THE MAGIC ALLEY

AN ALLEY THAT MAGICALLY MAKES THINGS BIGGER

1. Press out the alley and fold it as shown. Fold and glue the two figures and place in position.

2. Which figure looks bigger?

WOW!

3. Now swap them.

FOLD

FOLD

FOLD

FOLD

FOLD

DRAW YOURSELF HERE

FOLD

GLUE FLAP UNDER

GLUE FLAP UNDER

FOLD

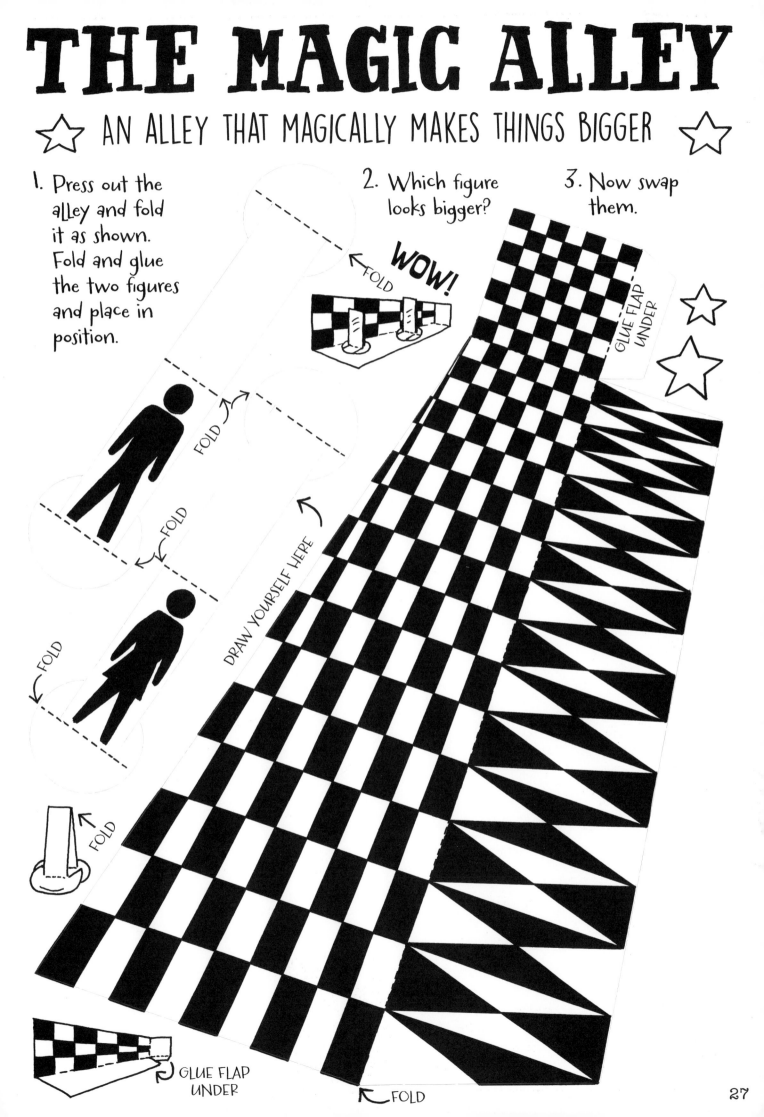

The design of the alley fools the brain into thinking the figure at the wider and taller end must be smaller, when in fact they are both the same size. This is a classic optical illusion.

Now see if the alley fools your friends.

THAUMATROPES

A thaumatrope is a simple toy that produces an optical illusion. To make some, press out the pieces, fold them, glue them to pencils and roll them rapidly between your hands. The images merge like magic.

Design your own T-shirt.

Draw your own emoji face.

WOW!

1. Place a pencil inside the press-out, fold and glue shut.

FOLD

GLUE

2. Spin it by rolling the pencil between your hands. You see just one magic image.

The guide on the next page will help you position your own images correctly.

WHAT'S THE SCIENCE?

FUN FACT:
The word "thaumatrope" means "wonder turner."

Thaumatropes have existed for almost 200 years.
They work on the principle of **PERSISTENCE OF VISION.**

When you look at something, your eye retains the image for a fraction of a second. If another image hits your eye in that time, then your brain combines them. That's what happens when you spin your thaumatrope.

Position your designs correctly by holding them against a sunny window. Draw inside the dotted lines.

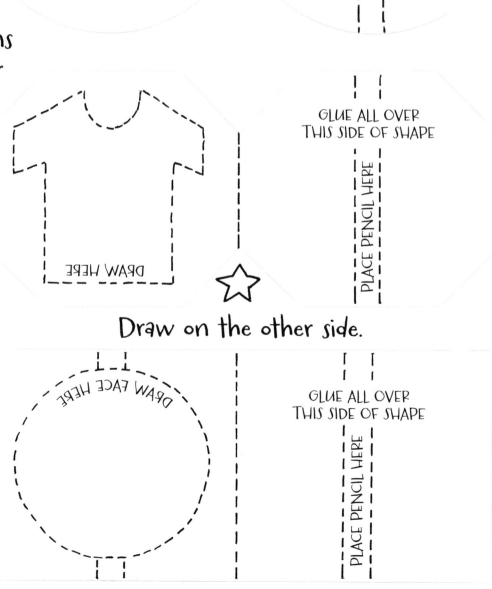

GLUE ALL OVER
THIS SIDE OF CIRCLE

PLACE PENCIL HERE

GLUE ALL OVER
THIS SIDE OF SHAPE

PLACE PENCIL HERE

DRAW HERE

Draw on the other side.

DRAW FACE HERE

GLUE ALL OVER
THIS SIDE OF SHAPE

PLACE PENCIL HERE

RINGS for WINGS

HOOP GLIDERS HAVE CIRCULAR WINGS—NOT FLAT ONES—BUT THEY STILL GLIDE BEAUTIFULLY.

START ROLLING HERE ↗

1. Make the body.

Press out, turn over and color. Roll around a pencil to form the body (fuselage) of the glider. Glue to close, and remove the pencil.

DONE!

PUT GLUE HERE

BACK

FRONT

2. Make the wings.

Press out and color. Fold over and glue the end flaps to make a flat loop. Tuck the wing through to make a hoop.

3. Attach wings to body.

Fold the "front" and "back" tabs on the body over the wing hoops and glue in place.

FOLD

GLUE

← Finished glider

Rear wing piece

COLOR IN THE HOOP WINGS.

FOLD UNDER

GLUE TO OPPOSITE TAB

Front wing piece

FOLD UNDER

GLUE TO OPPOSITE TAB

HOW DOES IT FLY? →

Hoop wings are highly unusual. The word "plane" actually refers to the flat surface of a standard aircraft wing. As your glider has circular—not flat—wings, it isn't a plane. It is a mini-aircraft.

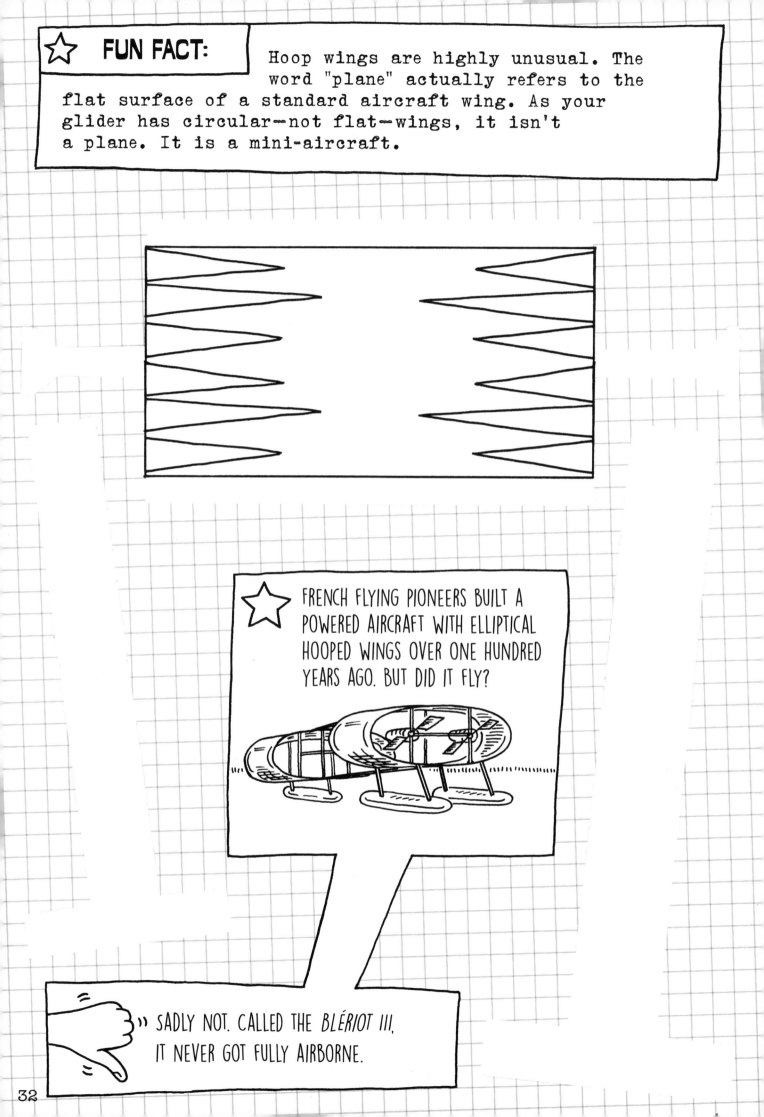

⭐ FRENCH FLYING PIONEERS BUILT A POWERED AIRCRAFT WITH ELLIPTICAL HOOPED WINGS OVER ONE HUNDRED YEARS AGO. BUT DID IT FLY?

SADLY NOT. CALLED THE *BLÉRIOT III*, IT NEVER GOT FULLY AIRBORNE.

Launch your glider with the small hoop at the front. Push it gently into the air and let go.

Adjust the sizes of the hoops (front and back) until the glider flies as far as possible.

HOW FAR CAN YOU MAKE IT FLY?

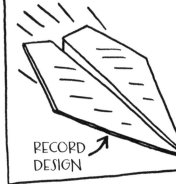

RECORD DESIGN

THE WORLD-RECORD DISTANCE FOR A FLIGHT BY A PLANE FOLDED FROM A SINGLE UNCUT SHEET OF PAPER IS OVER 225 FEET—ALMOST THE FULL LENGTH OF A JUMBO JET!

WHAT'S THE SCIENCE?

Your hoop glider is a mini-aircraft. Just as on a fighter jet, four forces act on it while it's in the air.

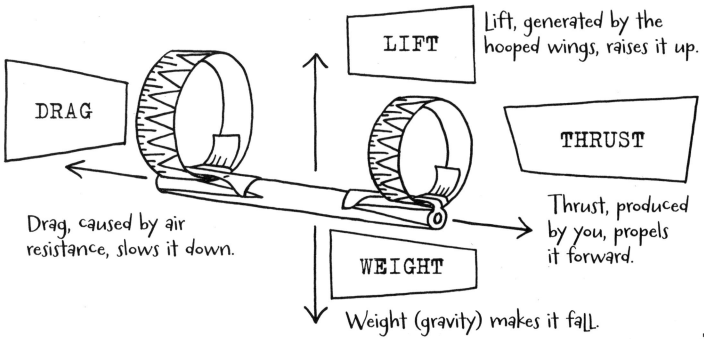

LIFT

Lift, generated by the hooped wings, raises it up.

DRAG

THRUST

Drag, caused by air resistance, slows it down.

Thrust, produced by you, propels it forward.

WEIGHT

Weight (gravity) makes it fall.

LIGHT SWITCH

Color the arrows in the strip below using blue for the ones pointing left and red for the ones pointing right. Color the other shapes in a mix of whichever colors you like. Next, fill a cylindrical, clear glass jar or bottle with cold water and view each strip through the glass. As you move the book farther away from the glass, something amazing happens—the arrows switch direction. Wow!

BUT WHAT HAPPENS TO THE OTHER SHAPES?

WHAT'S THE SCIENCE?

The water-filled container acts as a cylindrical lens that bends light passing through it toward a spot called its focal point. If you view each strip at a distance within the focal range, it looks "normal." But if it is beyond the focal point, the lens switches the sides around and the image reverses.

Color these red and blue.

These shapes switch direction.

These don't seem to. Why not?

Draw your own designs here.

BANG ✳ ON

MAKE YOUR OWN HANDHELD THUNDER CLAPPER.

This banging model uses just air to make a big noise.

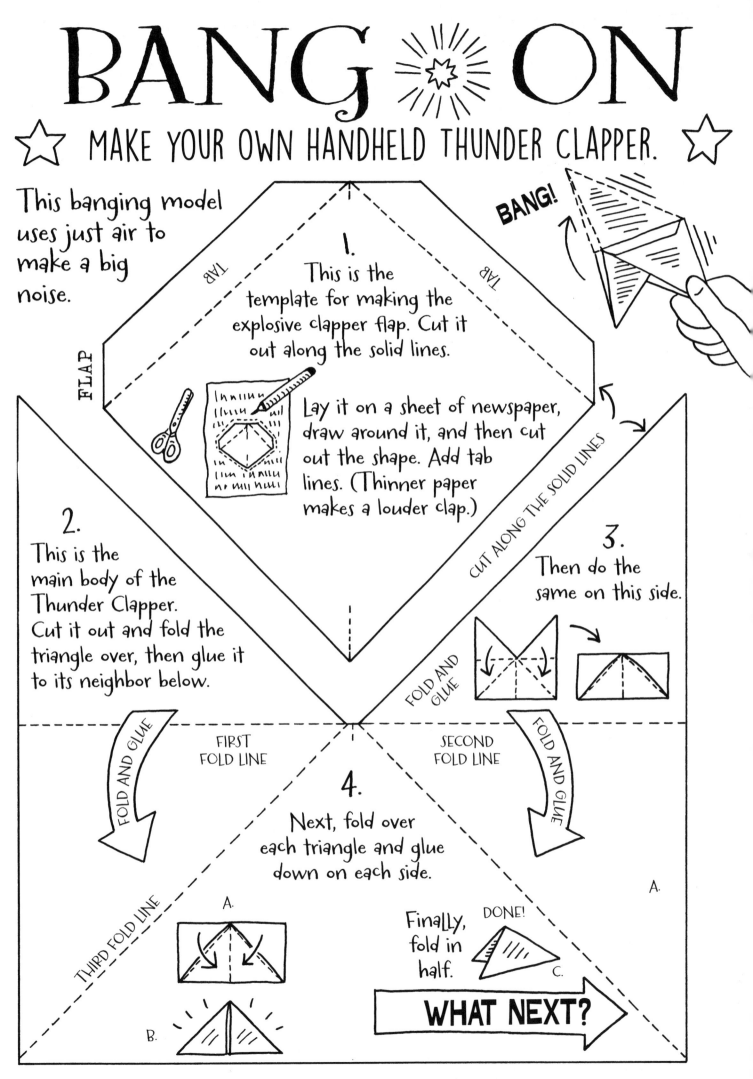

1.
This is the template for making the explosive clapper flap. Cut it out along the solid lines.

Lay it on a sheet of newspaper, draw around it, and then cut out the shape. Add tab lines. (Thinner paper makes a louder clap.)

TAB

TAB

FLAP

BANG!

CUT ALONG THE SOLID LINES

2.
This is the main body of the Thunder Clapper. Cut it out and fold the triangle over, then glue it to its neighbor below.

3.
Then do the same on this side.

FOLD AND GLUE

FOLD AND GLUE

FOLD AND GLUE

FIRST FOLD LINE

SECOND FOLD LINE

THIRD FOLD LINE

4.
Next, fold over each triangle and glue down on each side.

A.

B.

A.

Finally, fold in half.

DONE!

A.

C.

WHAT NEXT?

35

HOW TO ASSEMBLE YOUR BANGING THUNDER CLAPPER.

1. Fold the clapper flap in half.

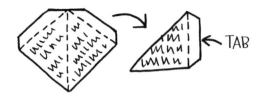

← TAB

2. Glue one tab to each side of the folded main body as labeled.

GLUE

FOLD IN

3. Prepare your clapper by folding the flap inside the body.

START POSITION

TIP: HOLD CLAPPER WITH A TIGHT FIST FOR LOUDEST BANG.

WHAT'S THE SCIENCE?

When you bring the clapper down quickly and with force, air resistance snaps the paper flap upward and outward. This action imparts energy to the surrounding air, which spreads out in the form of waves. When these waves hit your eardrums, your brain interprets them as sound. BANG!

BANG!

1. Bring your wrist/arm down with force.

2. Paper clapper snaps upward.

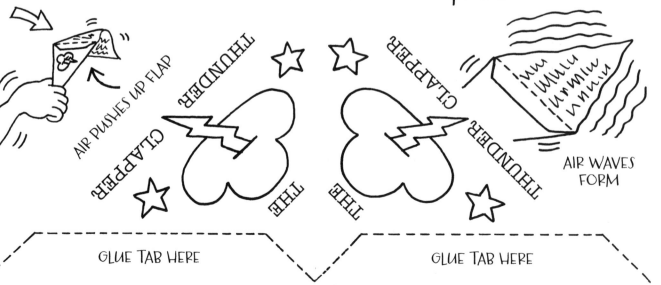

AIR PUSHES UP FLAP

AIR WAVES FORM

THE THUNDER CLAPPER

THE THUNDER CLAPPER

GLUE TAB HERE

GLUE TAB HERE

THE CURIOUS MOUSE

SEEING ISN'T ALWAYS BELIEVING, AS THIS ODD LITTLE MOUSE WILL REVEAL.

Carefully cut out the pieces along their solid outlines, color (if you'd like), then make your mouse as shown below.

1. Curl and glue the head to form a cone with the face inside.

GLUE

EASY!

← FOLD

GLUE UNDER

GLUE THIS TAB TO NECK

2. Fold and construct the body, then glue the head to the neck.

GLUE

DONE!

GLUE TABS UNDER

3. Now close one eye and look into the mouse's face.

GLUE UNDER

GLUE UNDER

IT'S SPOOKY!

THE

CURIOUS MOUSE

NEXT!

Try moving and tilting the mouse while still keeping one eye shut. The mouse will seem to look up, down, left and right.

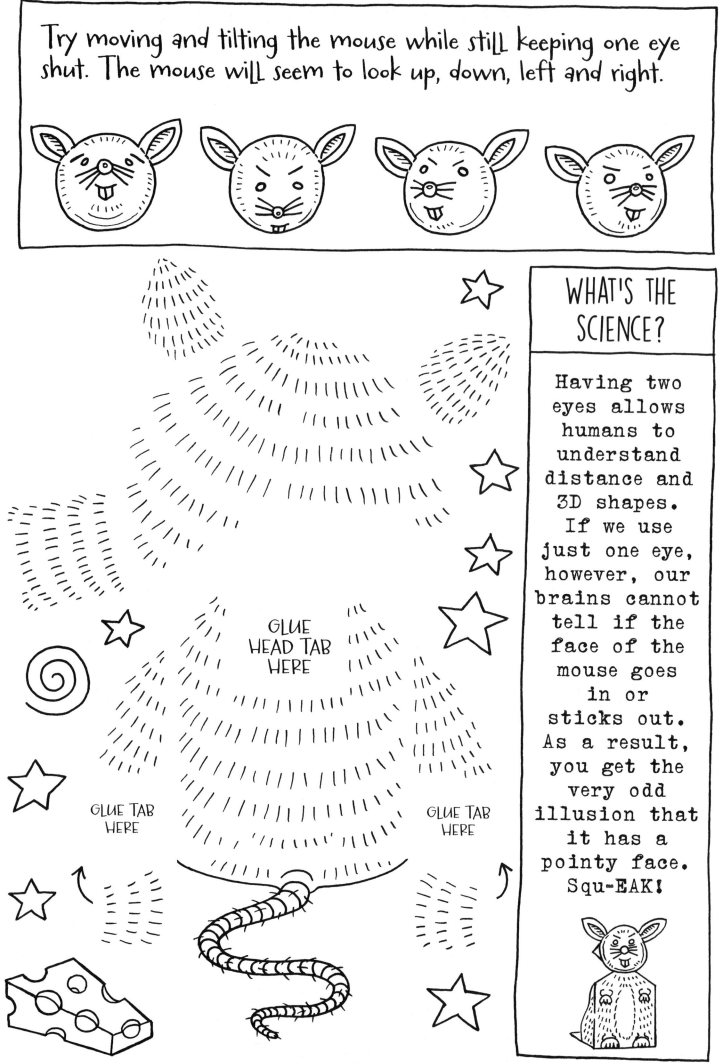

GLUE HEAD TAB HERE

GLUE TAB HERE

GLUE TAB HERE

WHAT'S THE SCIENCE?

Having two eyes allows humans to understand distance and 3D shapes. If we use just one eye, however, our brains cannot tell if the face of the mouse goes in or sticks out. As a result, you get the very odd illusion that it has a pointy face. Squ-EAK!

DOUBLE VISION

MAKE THINGS MOVE USING JUST YOUR EYES!

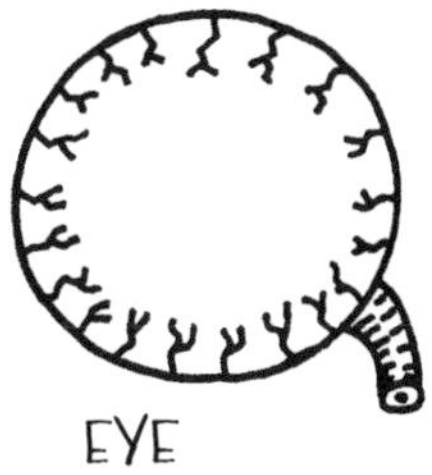

EYE

JAIL

CAT IN

LOVE

1. Fold the page on the dotted lines like this:

2. With both eyes open, bring your nose down over the ridge.

3. The images on either side will seem to move and combine.

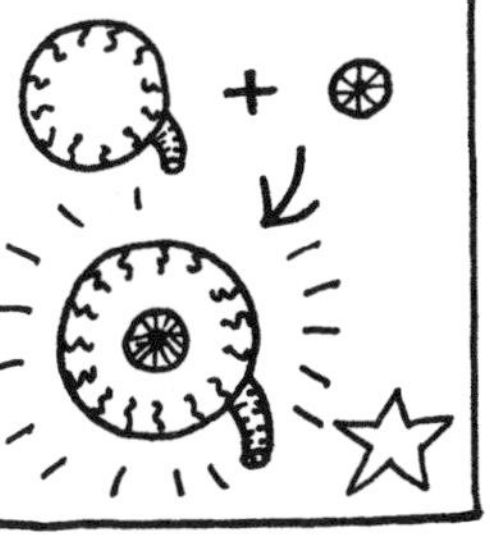

4. Draw your own pictures in the empty spaces below and label them.

WHAT'S THE SCIENCE?

Each of your eyes sends a separate image to your brain. The brain then combines the two images into just one. This is called binocular vision.

BALL

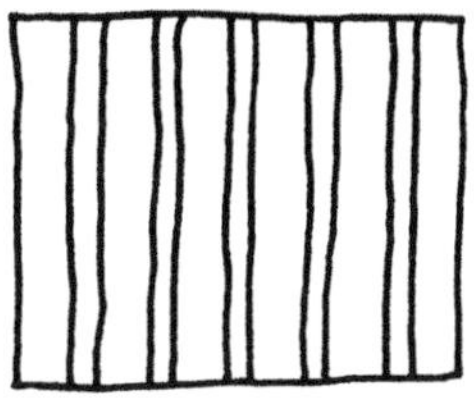

BIRD

A HAT

HEARTS

NO. 3: MARIE CURIE

Pierre and Marie, 1903

Marie Curie grew up to be one of the world's greatest Science Superstars despite not being allowed to study science in her own country because she was a woman. . . . Boo!

Born Maria Skłodowska in

Poland in 1867, she went to study in France, where she became the more French-sounding "Marie." Voilà!

She married a fellow scientist, Pierre Curie, in 1895, and their joint research into radiation won them the Nobel Prize in Physics in 1903. This made Marie the first woman ever to win a Nobel Prize. Hooray!

Marie and Pierre worked with the radioactive elements polonium and radium. Both are highly dangerous and later made Marie very sick.

MARIE'S OLD LABORATORY NOTEBOOKS ARE STILL HIGHLY RADIOACTIVE AND WILL BE FOR HUNDREDS OF YEARS!

NOW MAKE YOUR OWN MINI MARIE CURIE.

FUN FACT:

Marie Curie is the only person to win Nobel Prizes in two different sciences—chemistry and physics.

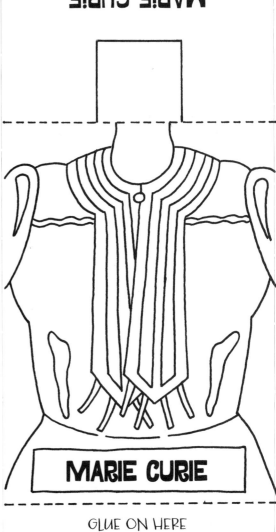

(PHYSICIST/CHEMIST)
BORN: POLAND, 1867
DIED: FRANCE, 1934

MARIE CURIE

MARIE CURIE

GLUE ON HERE

GLUE

GLUE TO HEAD ON REVERSE SIDE

Color the pieces, then press them out. Fold and glue the body into a triangle shape. Glue arms inside body. Attach head using neck piece.

GLUE TO BACK

Ra 88
Radium

GLUE

1.

2. GLUE

NOD!

3.

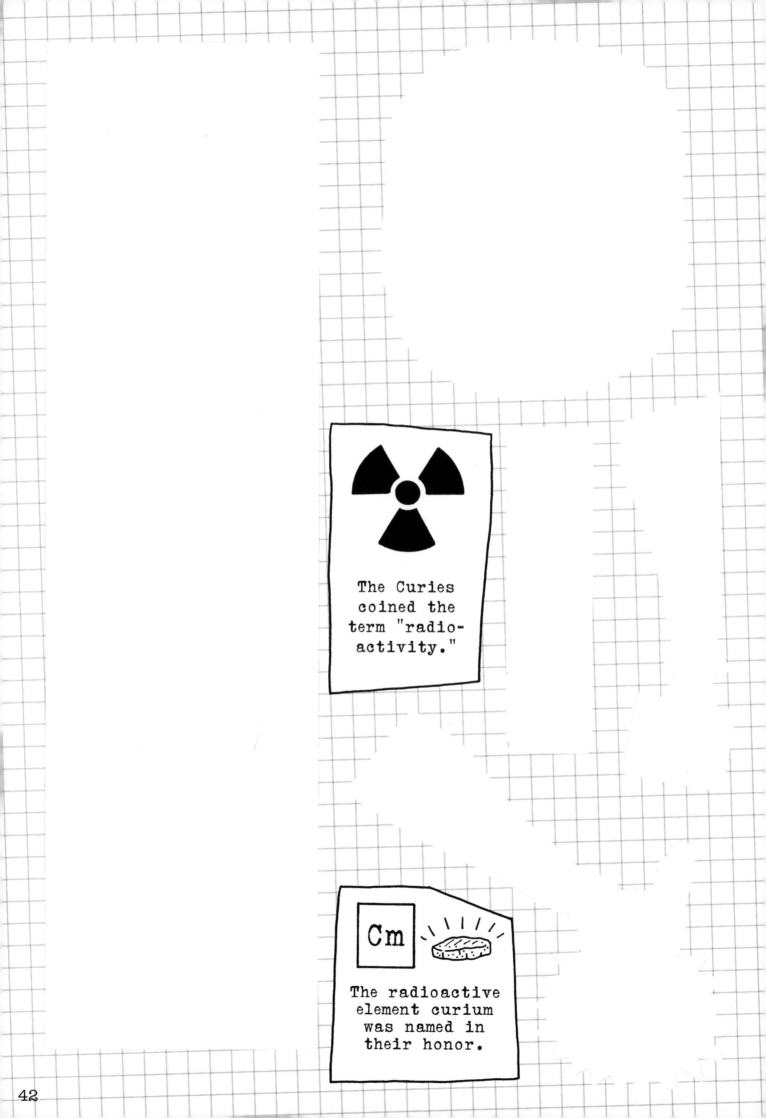

The Curies
coined the
term "radio-
activity."

The radioactive
element curium
was named in
their honor.

IN A SPIN

Press out, color and draw on the disks as instructed and place them on your Benham's top (see page 15).

What do you see when you spin them?

Color one of the spirals red and spin it. The effect is eye-bending!

Shade each stripe a different color. What do you think you will see?

NEWTON COLOR WHEEL

RED

ORANGE

VIOLET

YELLOW

INDIGO

GREEN

BLUE

"White" light is actually a mix of visible light, including all the colors of the rainbow. If you color in these sections and spin the disk, they should blend to give you a sort of muted off-white!

MORE

You can make your own rainbow at home by shining a flashlight onto a mirror angled in a dish or bowl of water. The light splits into seven visible colors!

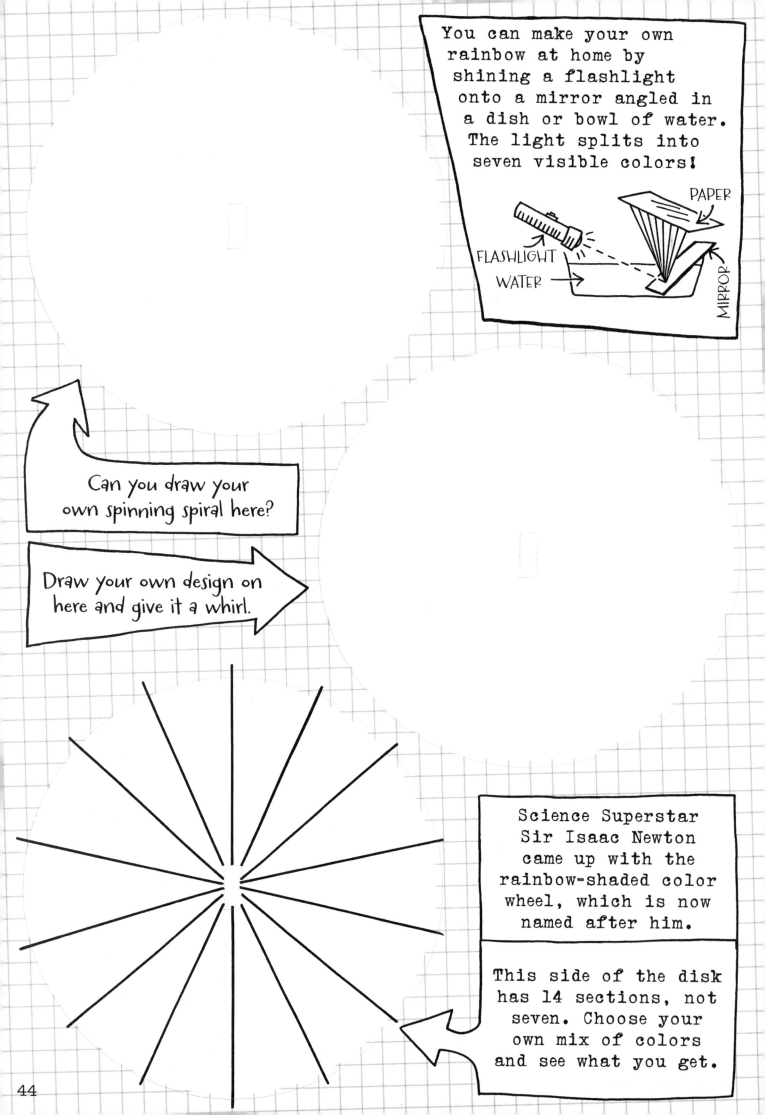

PAPER

FLASHLIGHT

WATER

MIRROR

Can you draw your own spinning spiral here?

Draw your own design on here and give it a whirl.

Science Superstar Sir Isaac Newton came up with the rainbow-shaded color wheel, which is now named after him.

This side of the disk has 14 sections, not seven. Choose your own mix of colors and see what you get.

BOOM TIME

MAKE MINI-BOOMERANGS THAT ACTUALLY RETURN.

Press out the two mini-boomerang models. Then color in or doodle on them and follow the simple instructions below.

1. Fold wing under.

Then fold tabs under, too.

2. Squeeze wing gently with your fingers and glue or tape tabs together to hold in place.

GLUE OR TAPE

3. The finished boomerang should have a curved upper surface and a flat lower surface.

FINISHED CROSS SECTION OF WING

THIS SPECIAL WING SHAPE IS CALLED AN AIRFOIL.

FOLD UNDER
FOLD UNDER
FOLD UNDER
FOLD UNDER
FOLD UNDER
FOLD UNDER
GLUE
GLUE

4. How to launch your boomerang:

Rest it on the back of your hand and flick it forward and upward on one side.

FOLD UNDER
FOLD UNDER
FOLD UNDER
FOLD UNDER
GLUE
GLUE

The oldest known boomerangs are over 10,000 years old.

HOW DOES IT FLY, AND WHAT'S THE SCIENCE?

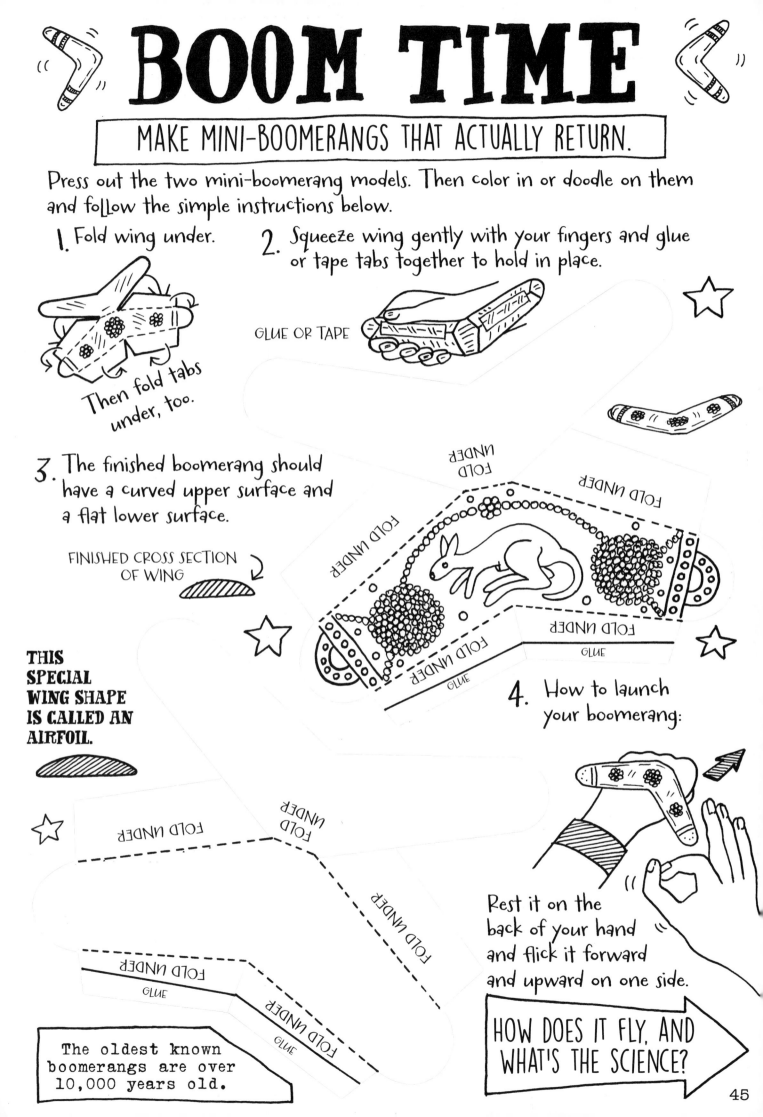

Your boomerang becomes a zoom-erang! Flicking the wing sets it off on a spinning flight that first takes it away from you, then sees it return in your direction.

With practice, you should be able to make it land at your feet every time. The special airfoil shape of the wing gives it lift, and the spinning action brings the boomerang back.

FLICK

TYPICAL FLIGHT OF A BOOMERANG

Boomerangs are the oldest-known man-made flying objects and were first used as weapons and for hunting.

Whizz!

OUCH!

These models are known as "returning" boomerangs.

NEWTON'S TABLE

Press out the table and tablecloth below. Add two coins—one big, one small—and you can do tricks with physics.

COLOR IN THE TABLE.

Table foot

Table piece

FOLD   FOLD   FOLD   FOLD

Floor piece

GLUE TABLE "FOOT" HERE

GLUE TABLE "FOOT" HERE

1. Fold table piece.

2. Glue on to the floor piece.

3. How you assemble the trick:

SMALLER COIN

BIGGER COIN

COIN HERE

COLOR AND FOLD TABLECLOTH IN HALF. THEN GLUE TOGETHER.

WHAT'S THE SCIENCE?

THIS TRICK IS NAMED AFTER ENGLISH SCIENTIFIC GENIUS SIR ISAAC NEWTON. BORN IN 1643, HE LIVED FOR 84 YEARS. ISAAC EXPLORED MANY AREAS OF SCIENCE, INCLUDING LIGHT, MOTION, HEAT, SOUND AND ASTRONOMY. HE EVEN INVENTED A NEW FORM OF MATH.

IT ALL ADDS UP!

Some say Newton invented the cat flap, but that's purr-fectly untrue!

MEOW!

Some magic acts perform this trick on stage using a real tablecloth.

HERE'S WHAT TO TELL YOUR FRIENDS:

1. "Isaac Newton has come for pizza, so we have to set the table."

PUT TABLECLOTH ON TOP OF THE TABLE.

2. "When the pizza is ready, it goes on a plate in the center of the table."

PUT COINS ON CLOTH, SMALLEST ON TOP.

3. "BUT Isaac HATES tablecloths, so we have to remove it quickly—before the pizza gets too cold."

FLICK!

Steady the table with one hand and sharply flick the tablecloth away with the index finger of the other.

Do it right and the cloth flies off, leaving the coins in place on the table.

The coins stay on the table due to "inertia" (in-er-shuh). Inertia is the tendency of objects to stay as they are—still or moving—unless a force acts on them. Isaac Newton described this in 1687, in his First Law of Motion. The friction between the cloth and the coins is not enough to move the coins, so they stay put.

FOLDED FACES

Tear out page and color the segmented faces using two different colors for the strips marked ● and ○. Then fold the page along the dotted lines like this:

⭐ When you view the strips from opposite directions, you will see two different expressions.

WHAT'S THE SCIENCE?

This ridged mix of images is known as a lenticular. Light travels in straight lines, so the images combine correctly only when they are directly facing you.

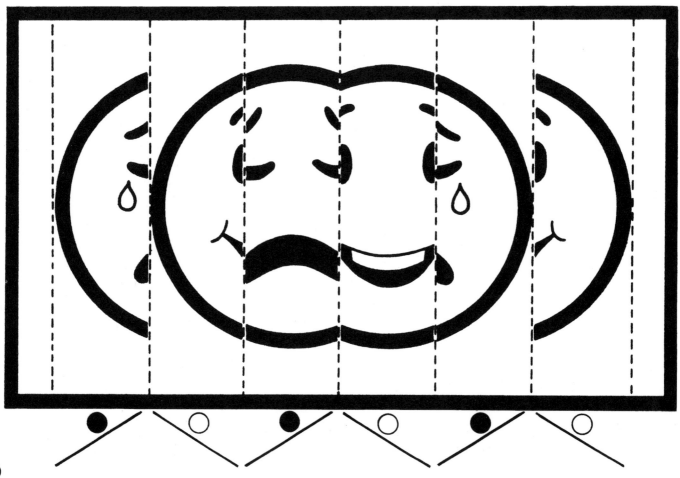

☆SUPER-FLY☆

YOU SHOULD GET A REAL BUZZ OUT OF FLYING THIS KITE.

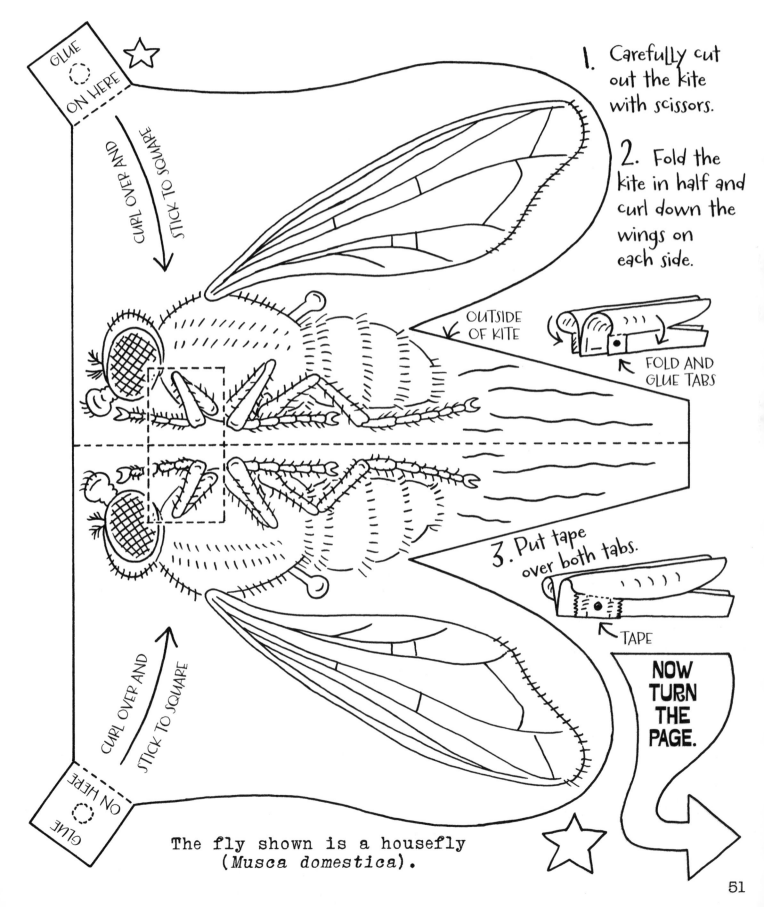

GLUE ON HERE

CURL OVER AND STICK TO SQUARE

1. Carefully cut out the kite with scissors.

2. Fold the kite in half and curl down the wings on each side.

OUTSIDE OF KITE

FOLD AND GLUE TABS

3. Put tape over both tabs.

TAPE

NOW TURN THE PAGE.

CURL OVER AND STICK TO SQUARE

GLUE ON HERE

The fly shown is a housefly (*Musca domestica*).

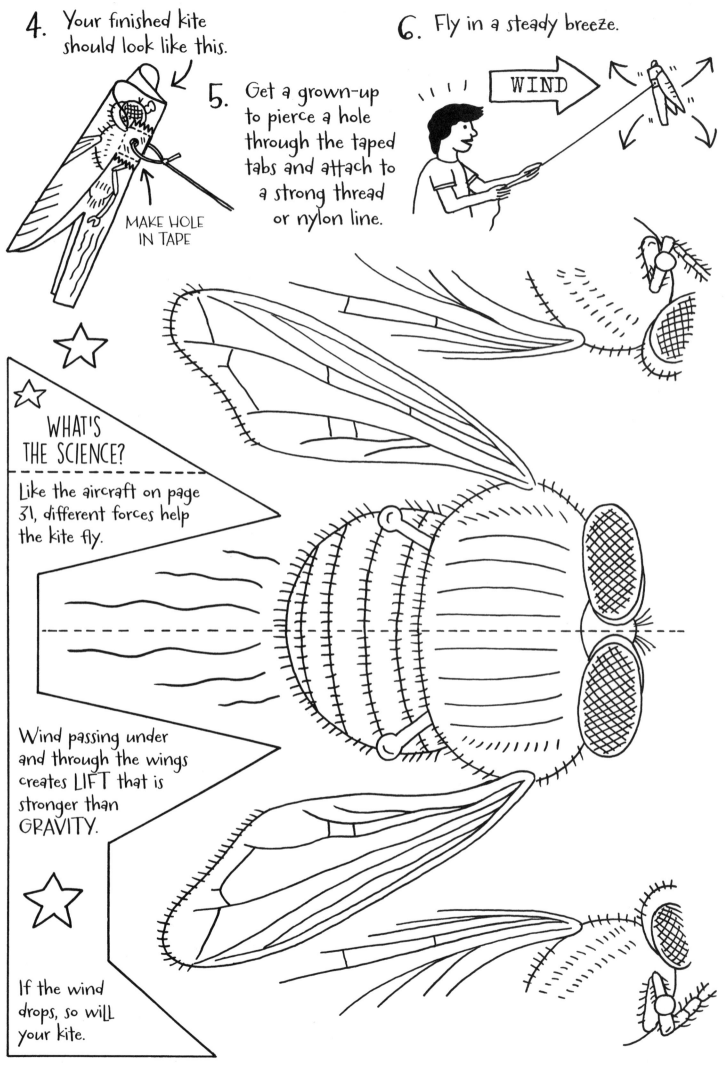

4. Your finished kite should look like this.

MAKE HOLE IN TAPE

5. Get a grown-up to pierce a hole through the taped tabs and attach to a strong thread or nylon line.

6. Fly in a steady breeze.

WIND

WHAT'S THE SCIENCE?

Like the aircraft on page 31, different forces help the kite fly.

Wind passing under and through the wings creates LIFT that is stronger than GRAVITY.

If the wind drops, so will your kite.

POLE POSITION

Cut out the pieces below along the solid lines to construct a "viewer." Color alternate diagonal stripes on the strip red, and insert it into the viewer. Slowly slide the strip in and out of the folded viewer and watch what happens.

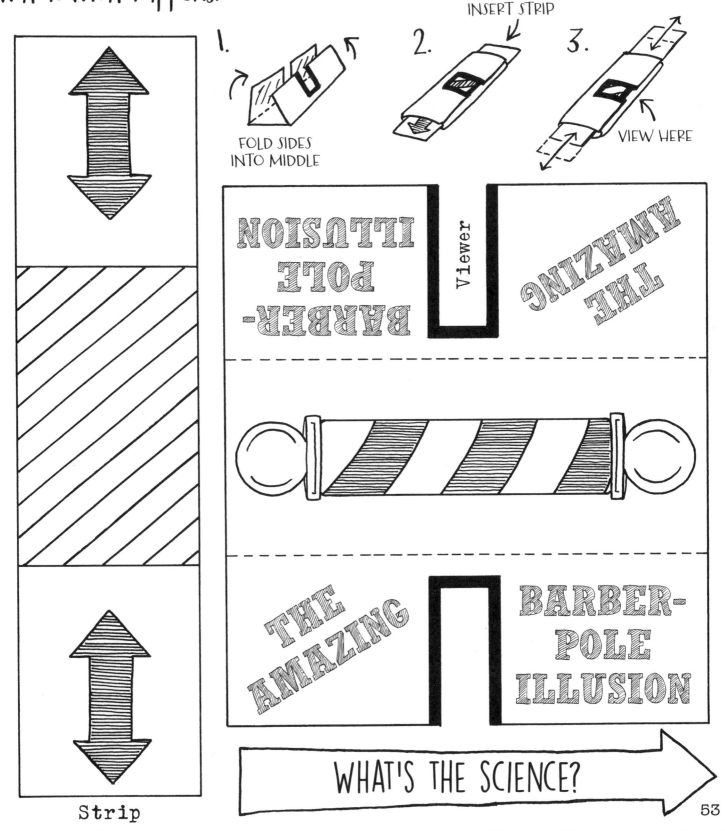

1. FOLD SIDES INTO MIDDLE

2. INSERT STRIP

3. VIEW HERE

Strip

Viewer

BARBER-POLE ILLUSION

THE AMAZING

THE AMAZING

BARBER-POLE ILLUSION

WHAT'S THE SCIENCE?

WHAT YOU SHOULD HAVE SEEN:

1.	SLIDE THE STRIP TO THE RIGHT.	2.	THE STRIPES SEEM TO MOVE UPWARD.	3.	SLIDE THE STRIP TO THE LEFT.	4.	THE STRIPES SEEM TO MOVE DOWNWARD.

THIS IS CALLED **THE BARBER-POLE ILLUSION.**

It happens because the narrow window of the viewer doesn't give the brain enough information to correctly interpret the movement of the stripes. Instead, your brain gives you its best guess.

FUN FACT:

Barber poles have red and white stripes to represent blood and bandages. This is because barbers used to perform surgery.

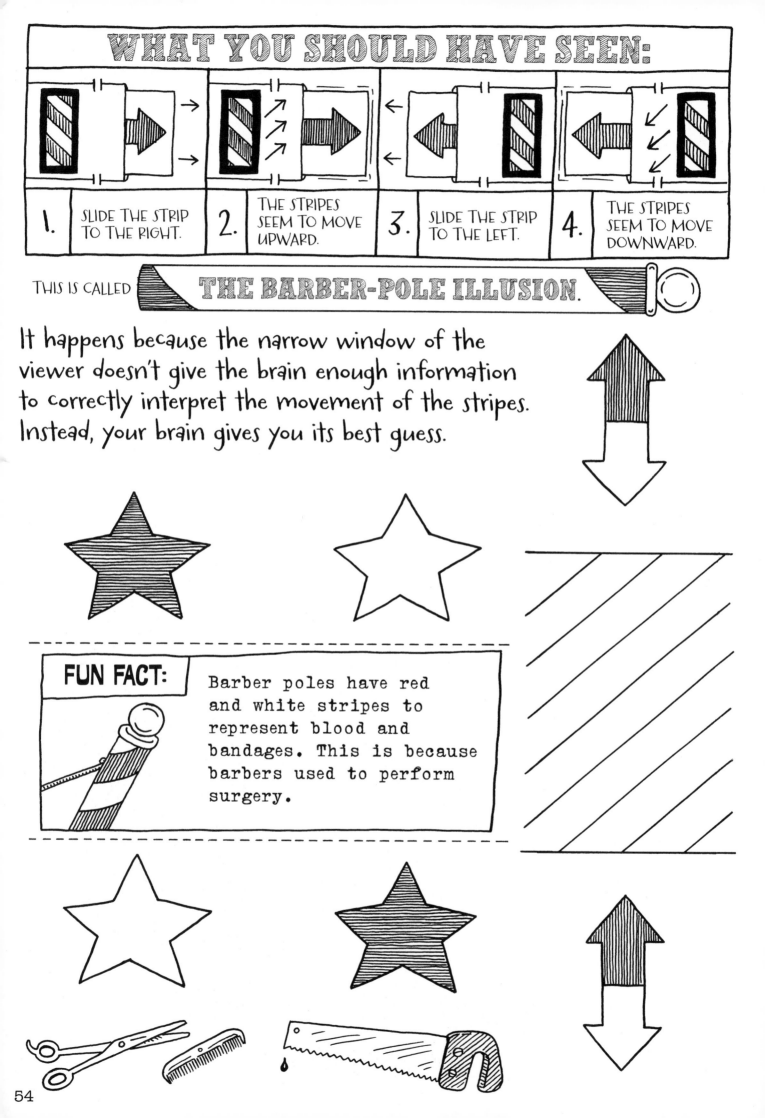

DO YOU DARE TO JOURNEY INTO A
BLACK HOLE?

Black holes are brain-boggling. They are not actual holes in space but defined areas made of super-dense matter, often the result of stars dying. Their massive gravitational pull means they suck in anything that comes too close—including light—and nothing ever escapes.

SO, DO YOU DARE TO ENTER THIS BLACK HOLE?

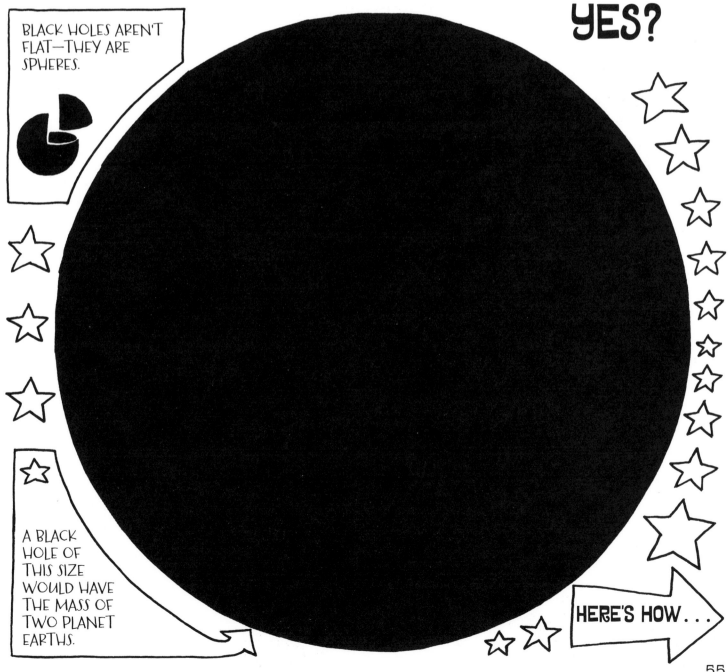

BLACK HOLES AREN'T FLAT—THEY ARE SPHERES.

YES?

A BLACK HOLE OF THIS SIZE WOULD HAVE THE MASS OF TWO PLANET EARTHS.

HERE'S HOW...

1. Cut out the black hole and fold it in half with the dashed lines on top.

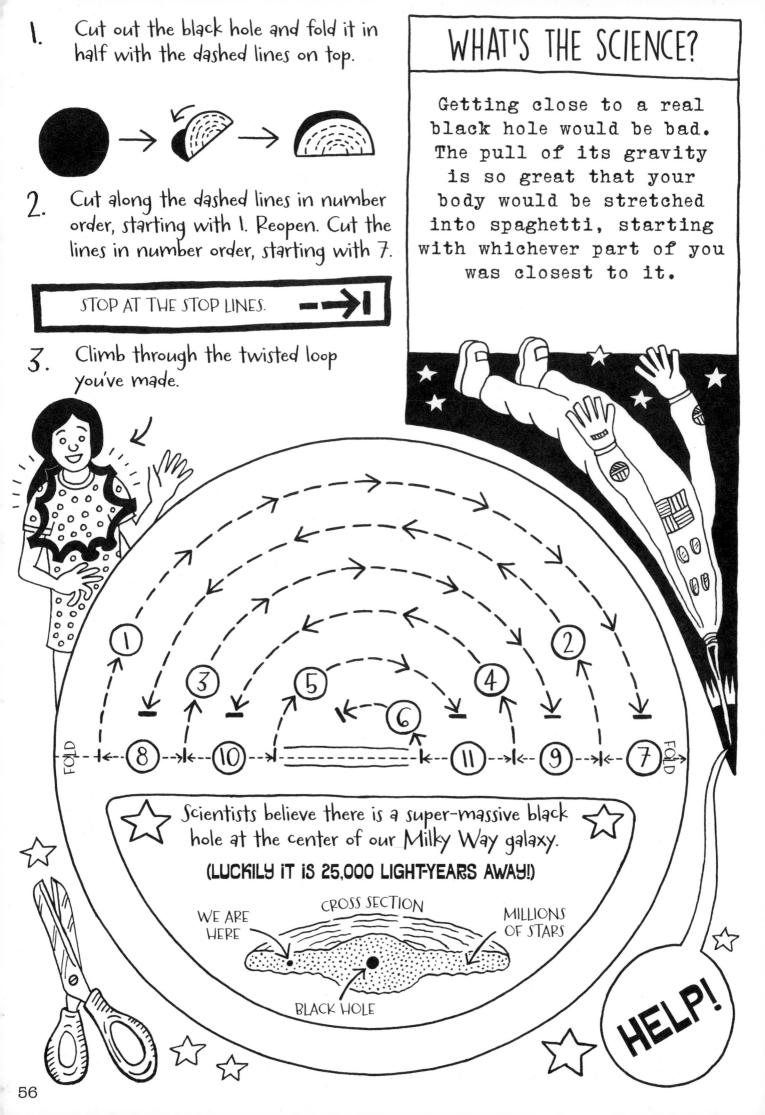

2. Cut along the dashed lines in number order, starting with 1. Reopen. Cut the lines in number order, starting with 7.

STOP AT THE STOP LINES. -- →|

3. Climb through the twisted loop you've made.

WHAT'S THE SCIENCE?

Getting close to a real black hole would be bad. The pull of its gravity is so great that your body would be stretched into spaghetti, starting with whichever part of you was closest to it.

① ② ③ ⑤ ④ ⑥ FOLD ⑧ ⑩ ⑪ ⑨ ⑦ FOLD

Scientists believe there is a super-massive black hole at the center of our Milky Way galaxy.

(LUCKILY IT IS 25,000 LIGHT-YEARS AWAY!)

CROSS SECTION

WE ARE HERE

MILLIONS OF STARS

BLACK HOLE

HELP!